Tips for Turnout

Written by Lisa Howell

Disclaimer

The contents of this manual, including text, graphics, images, and other material are for informational purposes only. Nothing contained in this manual is or should be considered or used as a substitute for professional medical or health advice, diagnosis, or treatment. The information provided in this report is provided on an "as is" basis, without any warranty, express or implied.

Never disregard medical advice from any treating doctor or other qualified health care provider or delay seeking advice because of something you have read in this document. We urge that dancers seek the advice of a physician or other qualified health professional with any questions they may have regarding a medical or health condition. In case of emergency, please call your doctor immediately.

The Ballet Blog holds no liability or responsibility for any injury or complication that may arise from following this information. Any use of this manual is voluntary and at your own risk. If you require further information about any injury, please feel free to contact us to organise an individual consultation either in person or via Skype/Phone.

Published 2019 by The Ballet Blog

© Copyright The Ballet Blog 2019

ALL RIGHTS RESERVED

Except for the purpose of fair reviewing, no part of this publication may be reproduced or transmitted in any form or by any means, electronic or mechanical, including photocopying, recording or any information storage and retrieval system, without prior written permission from the publisher.

Contents

Introduction	4
Part One - Achieving Your Ultimate Range	5
Find the Exact Point of Restriction	7
Mobilise	8
Why are the Muscles so Tight?	9
Part Two - Isolating Your True Turnout	10
Where are your Turnout Muscles?	11
How to Train Turnout Properly	13
Turnout Control in Standing	14
Turnout Exercise in Retiré	15
Turnout Control in a Tendu	16
Part Three - Achieving Ultimate Extensions	17
The Waiter Bow	19
Standing Iliacus Suck	20
Développé Devant In Lying	21
A Word to the Wise…	23
Related Resources	25

Introduction

Turnout - The elusive attribute that dancers seem to be either born with, or born without.

Ideally, if you are passionate about ballet you have the bony hip structure that lets you sit flat in second splits and easily stand in fifth position. However, so many of us do not have this natural facility, or struggle to control the range we do have. Does that mean we are all destined for a lifetime of struggling with our turnout?

Well, fortunately that isn't the case any more! The whole picture of "Turnout" is actually a whole lot more sophisticated, and a whole lot more promising than many of us thought for years.

The truth is that most of us have the capacity for a lot more turnout than we currently think we have. All it takes is a little education, a little understanding, and a little exploration, to start on the path to much happier hips!

Now "Turnout" is a rather huge topic, so this guide is designed to help you get the most out of your hips. The first part will be on how to increase your range of motion in various positions, the second will focus on strengthening the right muscles to actually use your new found turnout, and the third will be more focused on controlling turnout in your extensions.

Part One - Achieving Your Ultimate Range

Most of us aren't blessed with beautiful open hips from day one. If our hips are tight we usually try to fake it by forcing the knees back while dancing and gripping with the gluteal muscles. Unfortunately while many people try this strategy it is actually not very effective and usually ends up causing more problems than it solves. The same goes for stretching incessantly, perhaps even opening out your hips a little, only to wake up the next day stiffer than you were the day before.

So what is the issue with turnout? Why is it such an elusive quality and why are there so many myths about it floating around in the dance world? And perhaps more importantly, how can those of us with less than perfect rotation dance to our hearts desire without constantly irritating our hips?

From my point of view, as a physiotherapist who works with dancers every day, there are a few main categories of people who have issues with turnout.

1. **The "It-just-doesn't-happen" people:** With these dancers, no matter what stretches they do, their hips just seem to get tighter and tighter. They sit cross-legged and their knees go nowhere near the floor, and a lot of the time any stretches they try to do give them pain in the front of the hips.

2. **The "It's-OK-in-some-positions" people:** These dancers find turning out very frustrating.. Sometimes it's there and sometimes it's not. They may find it easy to sit in second splits, but struggle to stand in 5th position. Or they can hold it in 5th yet not in a développé devant.

3. **The "It-just-hurts-to-go-there" people:** This group may have good range, but whenever they try to train their hips, they seem to get more sore, especially in the front of the hips.

4. **The "I-just-need-to-crack-them-first" people:** This group will have a religious warm up that involves popping the hips either to the front or back to 'release' them before they can work in turnout. This may appear to work well for a while but often has diminishing returns. After a few months or years, the need to pop happens more often, yet the pops are often not quite as effective as they once were. The frequently popped area may start getting sore due to being repeatedly overstretched and unstable.

5. **The "I've-got-so-much-I-don't-know-what-to-do-with-it" people:** These dancers can also get very frustrated, as they are constantly told that they have great turnout, and can stretch into all kinds of wonderful positions, however they really struggle to show it when they are dancing, and often get told that they are just not trying.

So what is the solution? Do we all just give up and leave dancing to the ones who have 'natural turnout' and great control? Somehow I don't think that that is an option for all of the millions of us who love to dance despite not having the most open hips! Instead we must discover a way to train each individual's hips specifically, and to train dance teachers to be able to identify different types of hips early, allowing correct training of all students.

In the first stage we will be focussing on the first two groups of people described above, and on ways that you can improve your turnout range safely.

The first thing you need to understand is about the basic bony structure that gives our hips their stability. Most people know that the hip is a ball-and-socket joint, but they don't realise just how different everyone's ball-and-socket joints are. Some people have very deep stable sockets, some are more forward facing and some are more out to the side. Naturally open hips often have a shallow socket that faces more out to the side, but not always. The biggest problem is that most of us 'accept' that our range is blocked by the bones when this is actually not the case.

I had a massive rude awakening to just how much I had unconsciously accepted the fate of my not-so-flexible hips when at the ripe old age of 26 I had a massage that released lots of old, deep tension in my hips, giving me more range than I had at 16! This opened my mind to the possibilities for many other dancers, and lead to the development of a program to teach dancers how to open out their hips safely. (For more information on the Training Turnout Program visit www.theballetblog.com)

Find the Exact Point of Restriction

Many people blame the bony structure of their hips for a lack of turnout, but actually feel the block in muscular structures around the hips. When you go into a frog stretch, a grand plié, second splits or are standing in fifth, close your eyes and see if you can really feel what is actually stopping you from going further.

Is it:
- The front of the hip? (TFL?)
- Inside the hip? (Iliacus or Psoas Major?)
- The inside thighs? (Adductors and Pectineus)
- The sides of the hips? (Gluteus Medius and Minimus?)
- The back of the hip? (Hip Capsule or SIJ?)
- In your low back? (Lumbosacral Junction?)

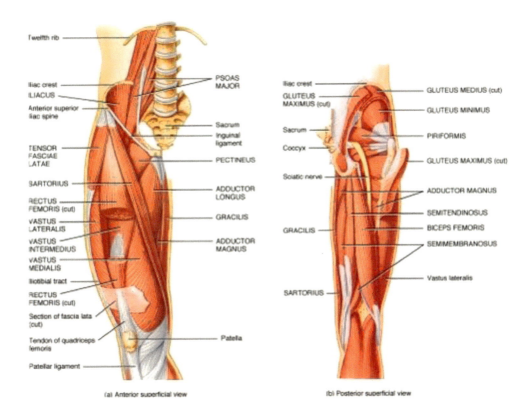

If you have access to a local Physiotherapist or Osteopath (preferably someone who works with dancers) they should be able to assess your hips in detail to work out where the blockage is. Dance Teachers who have completed my Level 1 Dance Teacher Training course will also know how to do this. Alternatively you can check up on the anatomical diagrams above to identify possible structures that may be blocking your turnout.

Mobilise

Now you may think that you have tried everything to open out your hips, but often the solution to your restriction is in the opposite direction to the goal when it comes to turnout. Once you have found the point of restriction that is blocking your range, the focus should be on releasing that structure, not necessarily into turnout. However once it has let go a little, you will find that it 'allows' more turnout in the positions that you need it.

Hip Flexor Mobilisers
One of the best ways of improving Standing Leg Turnout is opening out the front of the hip. Starting in a split stance with the back heel off the floor, mobilise the front of the hip by bending the front knee, sinking the back heel back, and keeping the front of the pelvis lifted. Aim to feel a gentle opening over a wide area instead of pain in the front of the hip. We have a video called "Safe Stretches for Tight Hips" on youtube that gives several other variations of this mobiliser.

Internal Rotation Stretch
Counterposing external rotation with an internal rotation stretch is very important in maintaining healthy hips. Keep the spine in neutral and walk the feet out to the side keeping knees together. Feel a gentle stretch through the outside of the hips. If there is pain in the groin or the knees do not do this exercise. Try tucking and tilting the pelvis to feel the stretch shift slightly. You can also allow the legs to gently drop in, alternating sides, to deepen the stretch.

Pretzel Stretch
This is a deeper stretch for the front of the hip that is great for mid to high level students. Start with the knees wider than the mat, and drop both knees to one side. Cross the right foot over the left knee and gently tuck and tilt the pelvis to mobilise the front of the left hip. If there is any pain in the knees work on the Hip Flexor Mobilisers for a few weeks before attempting again. Make sure that there is a support under the internally rotated knee if it does not easily reach the floor.

Why are the Muscles so Tight?

The main step in resolving restrictions around the hips is that people miss out this very important step. Any tension that is being held in your body is there for a reason, and the true 'cure' for improving your range is actually in identifying why those structures are getting tight in the first place. I commonly tell people that "The body is in a constant state of reformation" in that it is always adjusting and readjusting to the messages that you give it.

If you repeatedly clench a muscle, it may continue to hold tension long after it is needed. This can happen for many reasons, but most often it is due to chronic emotional stress, anxiety, trying too hard, compensation for other weaknesses or faulty technique, to name just a few. The following are some things to think about if you notice specific points of tension:

Adductors (Inner Thighs)
- Constantly crossing legs when sitting
- Overtraining one component (usually inner range strength) of the inner thigh complex (Yes you can do too many magic circle exercises!)
- Weakness of the stabilisers of the outside of the hip (Gluteus Medius)
- Weak Pelvic Floor (Causes Adductors to grip in an attempt to stabilise the pelvis)
- Emotional protection of the groin area (especially around teenage years)

Gluteus Medius (Side of Hip)
- Gripping with all gluteals to hold turnout
- Reduced isolation of true turnout muscles (Deep External Rotators)
- 'Sitting' into the hip
- Overtraining of Gluteus Medius in shortened or non-functional positions (i.e. Long Leg Lifts)

TFL (Front/Side of Hip) and Rectus Femoris (Front of Thigh and Hip)
- Overuse due to weakness of deeper hip flexors (Psoas Major and Iliacus)
- Poor Multifidus control (Deep Back Stabilisers)
- Reduced Pelvic Floor and Deep Abdominal control
- Weakness in Oblique Abdominals
- Hitching hip in Retiré and Développé a la Seconde

Once you can identify what is tight, and why it is tight, you will be armed with a completely new strategy to improving your turnout range. Please do not simply force the knees or hips open into classic stretches (froggy, side splits etc). These stretches do not usually help if you have a restriction in range, and sitting for long periods in these poses can actually damage the front of the hips.

Part Two - Isolating Your True Turnout

In Part One of this Tips For Turnout Series, we looked at ways of opening out the hips, to get some more turnout range, and discussed some reasons why your hips might be getting tight in the first place.

So now that you have a little more turnout range, how do you best work with it?

Once you have developed a little more range, it is essential to understand exactly how to train your turnout muscles safely. Far too many dancers do exercises to "improve their turnout" that may actually be damaging for their hips.

One of the most surprising things for us in the clinic is how few dancers actually know where their turnout muscles are! I always ask students to point out where their turnout muscles are both on their own body, and on a muscle chart and we always get a few surprising answers!

- Have a think about where you think your turnout muscles are.

- Do you know their names?

- What other muscles do you think help with turnout?

- What muscles should NOT be used? Why?

Where are your Turnout Muscles?

Your main turnout muscles are called your Deep External Rotators and they are located deep underneath your gluteal muscles. On this picture the big gluteal muscles (Gluteus Maximus and Gluteus Medius) have been cut away so that you can see the deep rotators.

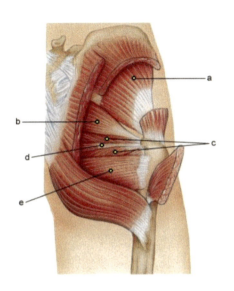

a. Gluteus Minimus
b. Piriformis
c. Gemelli (Sup/Inf)
d. Obturator Internus
e. Quadratus Femoris

There are actually six Deep External Rotators which are shown in the image above. Gluteus Minimus (a) is not classed as one of the deep rotators, but does help stabilise the hip, and actually assists in turning the leg in! The six deep external rotators are:
1. Quadratus Femoris
2. Piriformis
3. Gemelli Superior
4. Gemelli Inferior
5. Obturator Internus
6. Obturator Externus (Not indicated in image)

Each of these muscles works in a slightly different way, and in a different range. For example, your Quadratus Femoris is very much used in controlling turnout on your standing leg, whereas your Piriformis works more en fondu. In the Training Turnout program we go into how to train each of these muscles in detail.

So… Where are these muscles on you?
Your turnout muscles sit around the back of your hip, under the line of your leotard. The Piroformis extends from the lumpy bone on the outside of your hip (Greater Trochanter) to the front surface of your tail bone (Sacrum). Your Quadratus Femoris goes from your Greater Trochanter to your sitting bone (Ischial Tuberosity).

What other muscles do you think are involved in turnout?

Many people think that their bigger gluteal muscles, inner thighs or front of the hips are their turnout muscles. While the inner thighs do support turnout in some positions, they are not really 'turnout muscles'.

Your deepest core muscles are very important in creating a base to work your turnout from, and activity in the muscles in your feet can help stimulate a whole line of smaller muscles through your legs to stabilise more effectively in turnout.

Your deepest hip flexors (Psoas Major and Iliacus) are very important in helping to control the leg in turnout en l'air, and we will discuss this further in Part Three of this guide.

The inner part of the Quadriceps Muscle, VMO (Vastus Medialis Oblique) will help to control the alignment of the knee en fondu, but it is not technically a turnout muscle.

What muscles should NOT be used – and why?

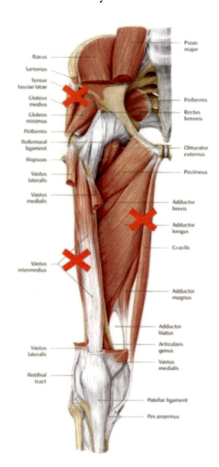

If you grip with all of your gluteals to try and hold turnout (especially Gluteus Maximus and Gluteus Medius) you will tend to develop a lot of tension in the gluteal area. This can restrict your flexibility into turnout and also into the splits.

Your gluteal muscles are important to help you jump, so if they are already being used for turnout, then they either won't be available to be used for jumping, or, if they let go of their job to turn out, then you will struggle to control your turnout in allegro. In addition, if you use your gluteal muscles or your hip flexors to help with turnout you may actually develop tension in these muscles that will REDUCE your turnout over time!

If you use the front of the hips to work your turnout, the TFL (Tensor Fasciae Latae) and Rectus Femoris will get very tight, and may become sore and inflamed. This is often felt with pain in the front of the hips with retiré or if you notice that the hips are very tight when going into a plié.

Also try not to grip with the outside of the lower legs when attempting to get more turnout. This puts a lot of strain on the ankle and knee, and can lead to all kinds of other issues!

How to Train Turnout Properly

Many people struggle to control turnout on their standing leg. This exercise is wonderful for not only finding your standing leg turnout muscles, but also helps in freeing up the range in this position. This exercise was developed to avoid all of the 'cheating' that goes on with other turnout exercises and has turned into one of our favourites!

Running Man Exercise

- Lie on your side with the underneath arm stretched out under your head
- Keep your hips square, and keep your hand on your hip to check that it doesn't move
- Place the knee and shin of your top leg on a pillow, supported at 90 degrees of hip flexion
- Make sure that the thigh of the underneath leg is in a straight line with the rest of your body, and the knee is bent
- Activate your deep tummy and back muscles, stabilising your spine in neutral
- Slowly rotate the thigh bone in the socket, taking the heel of the underneath leg towards the ceiling
- Keep the knee of the underneath leg in line with the rest of the body (it will usually want to creep forwards)
- Lift the heel as high as you can, without moving anything else, then slowly lower back to the floor
- Repeat between 10 – 20 times depending on your current strength

Training Tip
After doing one side only, come into standing and place the feet in first position. Try to rotate your thigh bone using the deep muscles that you felt working in the exercise. Note whether it is easier on the leg that you have just worked, Then try going into a plié, grand plié and a rise, maintaining your turnout from the hips.

Turnout Control in Standing

Once you have found your deep turnout muscles, it is a good idea to start to learn how to use them as you would in class. It is important not to grip the gluteals to achieve or maintain your range of turnout, but to isolate it from the top of the leg. For many more exercises designed to isolate your turnout in different ranges, please use the Training Turnout book.

- Begin by standing in parallel, then rock your weight back onto your heels
- Rotate the thigh bones, focussing on a deep rotation in the hip socket – using the muscles you worked in the first exercise - to take the feet into first position
- Place the front of your foot down in this position, ensuring the base of the big and little toes have equal pressure into the floor
- Make sure not to wiggle to get the feet out further!
- Prepare for a rise – by pressing the balls of the feet slightly into the floor – but still keep the skin of the heel touching the floor
- Use the tips of your fingers to check that the Gluteus Medius and Gluteus Maximus muscles are relaxed, while the Deep External Rotators are gently working to control the rotation.
- Lengthen the spine, imagining that you are growing 2 cm taller
- Slowly sink into a demi plié, staying relaxed through the front of the hips and glutes
- Check with your fingers that the Gluteus Medius is not gripping on too hard (a gentle tension is ok – constant gripping is not!)
- Make sure that there is an even fold in both hips and both knees (a lot of dancers have an uneven plié, simply through habit)
- Come into standing, maintaining rotation from the hip, gently activating the inner thighs and allowing the foot to return to neutral

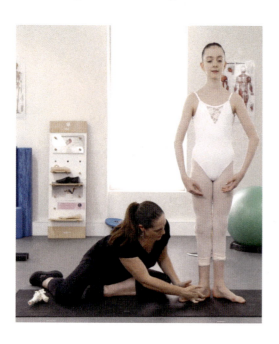 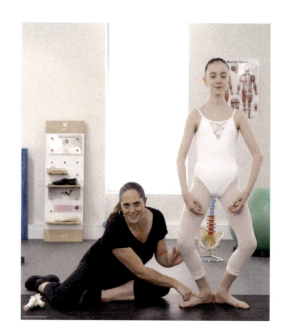

Turnout Exercise in Retiré

This is a fantastic way to find your turnout muscles while keeping the gluteals relaxed. Make sure you keep your deep core active, and that your back and hips stay still. If you have very tight hips or any pain in the hips, you may need to place a pillow under your pelvis for this exercise.

1. Lie on your stomach with your legs in parallel. Bend one knee to 90° and take it out to the side slightly. Loop a resistance band around your ankle, with the other end around a table leg or similar. Make sure that the resistance band is placed at an angle of 90° to your thigh bone.

2. Keep your hips in line (no hitching) and both hip bones on the floor. Have one hand under your forehead and the other on the upper gluteals of the bent leg to check for gripping.

3. Slowly bring the lifted foot towards the leg on the ground, as though you are going into a retiré position, against the resistance of the band. Focus on rotating the thigh bone in the socket using as little muscular effort as possible.

4. Pause, then slowly release the leg, returning it to the starting position. Repeat ten times on one leg, then repeat on the other side. Complete two sets of ten on each leg.

5. Make sure you are using your deep turnout muscles and not gripping with your outer bottom muscles. Remember to release SLOWLY, so that you are working the muscles on the way up as well as the way down.

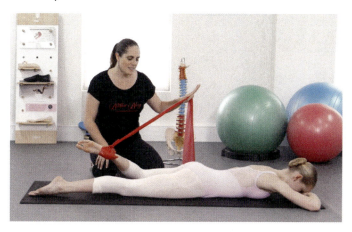

Training Tip
Test for over-activation of the Gluteus Medius and Gluteus Maximus by feeling for tension in the muscles along the top of the pelvis. The deep rotators are very deep and very small, so you may not actually feel them working strongly, however, if you are relaxing the outer gluteals, and still rotating the thigh bone in the hip socket, you are most probably using the right muscles!

Turnout Control in a Tendu

It is all fine and well working on your turnout in an exercise, however the real challenge is controlling turnout when you are dancing. Most people are focused on maintaining their turnout in their extensions (we will touch on that in Part three of this article) but the real secret is your standing leg. Far too many dancers focus on the working leg, yet you need a stable base to perform everything else off, so time spent on mastering the supporting leg is a very good investment!

One of the biggest challenges is to control the position of the supporting foot, and maintain turnout when on a single leg. Many dancers force their turnout when on two feet, and then let the heel slip out when going onto a single leg. This exercise can be very frustrating and a little demoralising when you first start it, but you will reap the rewards if you stick with it – I promise!

- Start in 1st or 5th position. Hands are on your hips initially, but can be held in first position or fifth position for a challenge later on
- Take care to have your feet in the 'Tripod Foot' Position, with the balls of the feet pressing slightly into the floor, yet keeping the skin of your heels touching the floor
- Focus on rotating the thigh bones in the sockets using the deep rotators and inner thighs
- Slowly release the front foot into a tendu devant
- Try and maintain the turnout of the supporting foot in the position it was in when in fifth position
- While the front foot is in dégagé, do a mini rise on the supporting foot to check your balance and weight placement, before lowering the heel
- Slowly return the working leg to 5th position, working the turnout of both legs
- Repeat three times devant, three a la seconde and three derrière before repeating on the other side.

Training Tip
The upper gluteals will work when on one leg. It is impossible to keep them fully relaxed so don't be too hard on yourself if this happens during this exercise. Make sure to keep the big toe of the working leg in line with the big toe of the supporting leg when working a la seconde.

Part Three - Achieving Ultimate Extensions

Do you constantly feel your hips and thighs gripping when holding extensions? Is your développé devant well off your full range of flexibility? Rest assured that if you answered yes then you are by no means alone, and yes, we have lots of tips to help you control your legs in higher ranges!

Many people focus on all the wrong things when they are trying to hold their legs higher so this section will help you get a deeper understanding of what to work on and how to do this in order to achieve your ultimate extensions! First of all, most people either focus on their flexibility alone, or work against resistance to try to lift their legs higher through brute strength. Neither of these strategies are very effective in achieving a beautifully controlled développé or arabesque. The following picture is designed to give you an understanding of all of the factors that combine to create the line you want.

Strength in the deep neck flexors to maintain softness in the neck and jaw

Thoracic mobility and control

Strength in the arm, yet softness in the wrist and fingers

Endurance in the deep back muscles

Turnout range and control of the lifted leg

Turnout range and control of the standing leg

Stability in the standing foot

Strong deep hip flexors (Psoas Major and Iliacus)

Strength in the knee extensors of the lifted leg

Inner thighs of the lifted leg

Flexibility of the hamstrings in turnout

Strength to keep the standing leg pulled up

Now that is a lot to take in all at once, so what do we work on first?

Believe it or not, one of the most important things in increasing the height of your extensions to the front is actually the strength in your deep back muscles. This is something that most people don't actually think to train when working on their extensions, but it can make a big difference to the height of your leg en l'air.

When lifting the leg devant, the main controller of the height of the leg should be your deepest hip flexor, Psoas Major. Unfortunately many dancers simply feel their quadriceps contract.

The Psoas Major attaches to the lowest four bones of your spine, and joins with another muscle - Iliacus - before attaching into the front of your thigh bone (Femur). The Iliacus sticks to the inside of your hip bone and is very hard to stretch effectively. Together these muscles form your Iliopsoas Tendon.

However – if the Psoas Major muscle is being used to stabilise the spine, it is less effective as a hip flexor, resulting in overuse of the other hip flexors, such as Tensor Fasciae Latae (TFL) and Rectus Femoris (RF).

Overuse of these two muscles is usually felt by gripping in the top of the hip (TFL) or excessive tension in the front of the thigh (RF) with your développé.

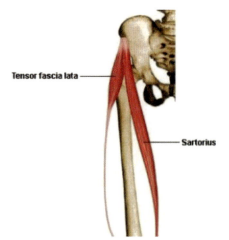

So how do we stop this from happening…?

Dynamic control in the deep stabilisers of the low back can help reduce the stabilising role of the Psoas Major Muscle, allowing it to function more efficiently as a hip flexor – resulting in:
- Less pain and gripping in the top of the hip
- Less tension in the thigh of the working leg
- Improved height of the leg en l'air
- More stability and control of the trunk during the movement.

One of the best exercises to really develop the control of these deep low back muscles in the way they need to work for a développé devant is with an exercise that we call the "Waiter Bow"

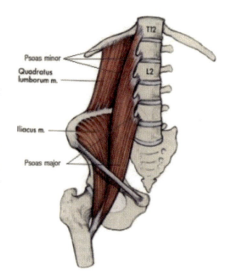

The Waiter Bow

This exercise really challenges the ability of your deepest back muscles to maintain the position of your back. It will also show you how mobile your hamstrings really are – and how much you tend to cheat range with your low back!

1. Stand side on to a mirror, with your knees slightly bent and your back in 'neutral spine' – with a tiny curve in your low back, but your upper back relaxed. Place one hand on your low tummy, and the other behind your low back to check that they both stay still throughout the movement.

2. Start tilting your body forward from the hips, maintaining your spine in neutral. This may take some practice to keep your low back in a good position, so be patient and precise!

3. Once you have the feeling of maintaining your low back position, and keeping the upper back relaxed, try tilting forward until the body is horizontal with the floor. This is harder than it looks! If you can do this easily with bent knees, try with the knees straight.

4. If you can go to horizontal easily, see how much further you can go while maintaining your back in neutral, without arching the upper back backwards or flexing the low back. Test and compare your range to your current height of your développé!

Training Tip
Also try this exercise with the feet in first position and see how different this feels. The further you can go with this exercise, the higher your legs will be able to come in your développé. If you are having to round out your lower back to flex forward, you will probably not have the mobility in the hamstrings, nor the strength in the lower back to hold your développé at the height you want it to be.

Standing Iliacus Suck

Next up is developing the strength to actually hold the leg in place. Once the deep back muscles are capable of stabilising the spine, you need to train the deep fibres of the Psoas and Iliacus to be able to hold the leg in position. To do this you must learn how to find the deep hip flexors, without over-recruiting the TFL or Rectus Femoris.

Before going into the Standing Iliac Suck it is a good idea to practice the lying version. Just do a couple on each side to activate the Iliacus before trying to recruit it in standing. Remember that Iliacus works subtly to draw the thigh bone back into the hip socket to give you more control of the leg en l'air and help offload the superficial hip flexors.

Lying Version:
- Lying on your back, with one foot on a chair or Swiss ball, making sure the thigh bone is vertical.
- Use your fingertips to feel the outside of your hip and top of the thigh to ensure these areas stay soft and relaxed.
- Visualise the thigh bone sinking deep into the socket and then gently float the knee towards you, keeping the spine in neutral and the TFL relaxed.
- Slowly release and return to the starting position.

Standing Version:
- Stand on the left leg and place the right foot onto demi-pointe. Stay lifted through the centre and lengthened through the sides of the waist.
- Connect the right hip bone deep into the socket with the Iliacus Suck, then float the thigh bone up towards 90°, maintaining natural breathing.
- Make sure to keep lifted through the tiny deep low back muscles, maintain neutral spine and don't tuck the pelvis. This will destabilise the lower back and put a lot of load into the front of the hip.
- Don't worry if the lifted leg doesn't stay parallel. With some anatomical variations it will deviate slightly into external rotation.
- Repeat on alternate legs, four to eight reps on each side depending on your current strength and endurance.
- As you get stronger you will be able to take the thigh bone past 90°. The higher you can take the thigh bone with the spine in neutral. the more effortless your développé devant will become!

Développé Devant In Lying

This exercise is very good way to refine your technique and correct any 'cheating' habits that you may have used in the past in an attempt to get your leg higher. Performing this exercise on the ground allows you to create a new movement pattern which is much more focused on centralising the hip, finding your deep rotators and flexing the hip using your Psoas Major. Combining these elements in sequence, but in a more abstract position, helps create a new motor pattern in your brain, rather than modifying your old one, which helps retrain your patterning for performing développé much faster. As there is less effect of gravity on the working leg, you can learn how to subtly coordinate the correct muscles around the hip to place the leg in a good position, so that when you return to standing, it is much easier..

Make sure you are nice and mobile through your hamstrings, and have woken up all of the deep core and hip muscles before attempting this. This is a really good exercise for those dancers who have lots of mobility but who struggle to control their leg at the front. It helps gather all the things we've been talking about in sequence so that you can transfer them directly into your dancing.

Level 1:
- Start lying on the ground, with feet in fifth position.
- Flex your supporting leg and keep the back border of the foot engaged with the ground, so that your standing leg turnout muscles are working.
- If you do not have the available range to have the foot flat to the floor, simply visualise this, and make sure to keep the deep rotators engaged throughout.
- Slowly peel the right leg up into a retiré focussing on keeping flat through the hips.
- Make sure to use all available range through this movement, rather than lifting the leg in a turned in position and dropping it out in the retiré position.
- Slowly, unfold the leg to a développé devant at 90° making sure that the hips stay square.
- Rotate your leg into parallel and then back into turnout three times.
- Make sure to keep connected to your centre and use your deep hip rotators to isolate the leg in the socket.
- Slowly lower the leg in turnout, then repeat on the other side.
- You only need to do one to two repetitions of each variation.

Level 2:
- Start as for Level 1, peeling up through retiré to a développé devant at 90°.
- Using your opposite hand, mount your lifted leg to where you'd like your développé to be.
- Take special note of your placement, keeping the thigh bone really rotated into the socket.
- Make sure you don't hitch the hip of the working leg up.
- Think of keeping a little lift through the low back to activate those deep muscles.
- Maintain a deep connection with your psoas from the front of the hip through to the front of the spine.
- Once you have found the correct position, slowly let go of your leg and see if you can maintain the position of the leg with your Psoas and Iliacus connection.
- Lengthen the back of the knee, keeping the whole leg nicely rotated and foot fully pointed.
- Hold for a breath or two, then lower the leg to the floor.

Level 3:
- Start as for Level 1, but as you unfold from the retiré, place your leg where you'd like it to be when standing.
- This will require a deeper engagement of Iliac and Psoas Major to place the thigh bone above 90°.
- Maintain the deep rotation in the socket, deep connection in the front of the hip, and unfold the leg keeping it in midline.
- Lengthen the back of the knee of the supporting leg and ensure turnout is maintained.
- Pause for a few breaths, before lowering the leg.

This exercise is more of a neural activation process than a loaded muscle exercise. It's more about learning how use your brain to connect to the required muscles rather than doing repetitions under load to create strength. When training the hip it's more about subtle coordination of all of the muscles around the hip rather than brute strength. There should never be any pain following any of these exercises but you will feel a lot more woken up around the hips and should feel more stable when you come to standing.

A Word to the Wise…

The other question that constantly gets asked in regards to all of the exercises that I prescribe is "When is the best time to do them?"

These exercises really can be done at any time during the day, however, a really good time is to go through them before class. After a quick warm up, do some gentle mobility exercises and short stretches to open out the hips. Please remember not to do stretches longer than 30 seconds before class, as sustained stretches can actually prevent the muscles from being able to contract properly.

Once the hips are feeling looser, go through the exercises in this program to 'wake up' your turnout muscles. You do not need to do many of each, but just focusing on them, and activating them before class, will make them much easier to find and use in class.

One other point to remember is not to try too hard when training your turnout muscles. Most people who struggle with turnout think that if they squeeze their muscles harder their turnout will get stronger but this usually actually makes the hips tighter. Turnout control is more about subtle coordination of the muscles around the hips, of using the most minimal amount of effort at just the right time.

Once you have developed control in all of these areas, you can start to take the leg higher devant without putting too much extra load on the other parts of the hip. Take this slowly but if you work on all of these areas you should start to see some major improvements in the height of your extensions!

For more information on controlling the leg en l'air please take a look at our Training Turnout, A New Approach to Core Stability, and Développé Devant programs, as all of these go into much more detail on how to master control of your spine, pelvis and hips in order to achieve your ultimate extensions!

Acknowledgements

Thank you so much to every single client I have ever worked with. Your uniqueness, challenges and feedback have helped me hone our programs to be the most effective and efficient way of dealing with common issues, with enough customisation to ensure great results for everyone.

Huge thanks must also go to the hundreds of dance teachers worldwide who have attended my Teacher Training courses, and given such positive feedback on the application of these programs. I thrive off the feedback you give me, and your infectious enthusiasm inspires me to keep on giving.

Lisa xx

Related Resources

How to Get Your Legs Higher in a Développé Devant

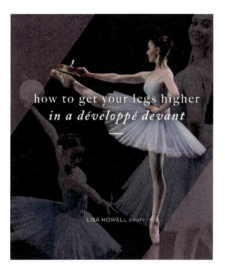

Welcome to our unique program which will teach you how to get your legs higher in adage, especially in a développé devant. Dancers all over the world ask how they can get their legs higher during adage, and the secrets to this are sometimes a little bit different than they realise. Many people think that if you apply resistance or put weights on your legs and practice the movement then it will get better, but unfortunately that often results in more load through the hips leading to increased tension, more restriction and frustratingly slow progress. Instead this program incorporates the latest research to get your legs higher to the front, including mobilisation techniques for enhanced flexibility, spinal and pelvic mobility and control, and detailed hip control in a specific sequence. It also introduces a concept of Mobilise - Isolate - Integrate - Function that can help you structure your conditioning programs for the best effect!

A New Approach to Core Stability

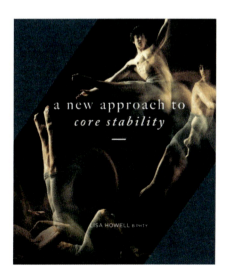

This book on "core stability" is based on evidence based medicine, and years of clinical experience, as well as the authors own journey with back pain. After being frustrated by the lack of resources that explained exactly what "core stability" is all about, and suffering back pain unnecessarily for years herself. She wanted to help everyone learn the secrets to get rid of constant nagging, and often excruciating back pain, and also be able to retrain their spine to be able to perform again at a high level, whether that be into deep back bends in yoga, running up stairs, managing 18 holes of golf or a 4 hour shopping expedition. This program demystifies the specifics of core stability that are essential in mastering control of your true core, and is essential to a full recovery from back pain, and has the added benefit of better performance of most sporting activities as well!

Made in the USA
San Bernardino, CA
22 January 2020